The Playing Card Workbook

The Playing Card Workbook

A Contemporary Manual of Cartomancy

by

Joanne Leslie

Illustrations by Linda J. Smith

THE AQUARIAN PRESS

First published 1988

British Library Cataloguing in Publication Data

Leslie, Joanne
The playing card workbook
1. Fortune-telling by cards
I. Title
133.3'2429   BF1878

ISBN 0-85030-743-0

*The Aquarian Press is part of the Thorsons Publishing Group,
Wellingborough, Northamptonshire, NN8 2RQ, England*

Printed in Great Britain by
Woolnough Bookbinding Limited, Irthlingborough, Northamptonshire

3 5 7 9 10 8 6 4

For my gardening instructor

Acknowledgements

To Patricia Allen for her generous help with the practical preparation of this manuscript, and to my sister, Emily Peach, without whose encouragement and supportive advice this book would not have been written. Thank you.

The author and publisher are greatly indebted to Waddingtons Games Limited for permission to reproduce their playing cards which are illustrated in this book.

Contents

Introduction

On numerous occasions, clients coming to me for a reading for the first time have expressed surprise that I work — as I have for some years — with playing cards. In the eyes of the general public these cards are obviously looked upon as being purely for games of chance.

Their original use was in fact for divination — looking into the future — and it is only comparatively recently that this has given way to the now more common use in gambling.

Over the past few years public interest in all forms of divination has grown, and playing cards are again coming into their own. The aim of this book is to show the beginner, in a clear and simple way, how playing cards can be used very effectively to assess people, both in character and potential, and — with their permission and co-operation — to look into their future.

1

Beginnings

Some years ago, while rummaging in the attic of my parents home, I found a book which had belonged to my grandmother, a book which was to play quite a large part in changing the pattern of my life. Called *Everything Within*, it covered everything from bricklaying to spot removal, but its most interesting section for me was the chapter devoted to 'Fortune Telling'; astrology, palmistry, tea leaves — and playing cards.

Like most people I had always been interested in clairvoyance, perhaps more so because most of the females in my family had demonstrated one form of psychic ability or another. However, in common with the majority of the population, I had looked on playing cards as being used solely for games of chance or patience. The prospect of 'telling fortunes' with them fascinated me, and for some months my friends and I played with the book and a pack of cards in much the same way that I imagine you are going to play with this book and your own cards.

My book, already very old, fell apart with the strain of being carried around in my bag, leaving me with just the relevant pages — and the interest, which never waned. When some time later, I commenced serious psychic development, it was with the alternative divinatory Tarot cards, but I soon drifted back to my dog-eared pages and my playing cards, although now in a much more committed way.

Human beings are always getting gentle pushes in the right direction, so I think I was intended to find that old book that day. Undoubtedly both book and cards have forged a very important link in my life in aiding development of an interest which rapidly became a way of life.

Perhaps you were intended to have *this* book for much the same reasons. Only time will tell . . .

2

Buying and preparing your cards

Before you can go any further, it is necessary for you to buy a pack of playing cards and keep them exclusively for the purpose of this study. The special purchase of a pack indicates your willingness to learn and gives a nice 'new feeling' start to the project.

There are quite a few different types of playing card on the market, some of them very pretty. I have always felt that, if one is going to spend a lot of time with an object, it should be as attractive as possible, so look around and get whichever type takes your fancy. If I may, I would like to offer just a couple of guidelines. Cards with the denomination printed in each corner (as shown below) are the easiest

to use, because you will be able to see instantly what they are, even if they happen to be partly obscured by other cards. I do *not* however, recommend that you use plastic cards. They last for ever of course, but they are far too thin and slippery, and particularly for a beginner this makes them very difficult to handle. One can feel very silly if they slip in the middle of a solemn shuffling process, resulting in one grovelling on the floor for missing cards.

2

I shall be referring to the cards as tools, and that is exactly what they are. The possession of tools makes you a craftsperson, and like all craftspeople you should learn to respect your tools and care for them. For this reason you should not allow other people to handle your cards except when you are attempting to do a reading for them. The cards should preferably be kept in a small wooden box when not in use, and (horror of horrors!) they should *never* be used for playing games of any kind.

All of this may seem to you like unnecessary mumbo jumbo, and how much of it you follow will depend on how seriously you intend to learn. All I will say on this at present is that the act of sitting down and taking your own special cards out of their own special box will help to put you in the right mood to carry out a reading.

When you have bought your chosen cards, take a really good look at each one. At this stage most of them will look appallingly similar, but the picture (or 'court') cards have a great deal of detail on them which you have probably not noticed before. Any detail is going to be useful to you when it comes to remembering what each card represents, so this familiarization with the cards is well worth your while.

For example, take a good look at the Kings, and particularly look at their hands. On three of them, Diamonds, Clubs and Spades, most packs will show the King as having just one hand showing at each end of the card. The exception is the King of Hearts with a total of four hands — two at the top and two at the bottom. Now the King of Hearts is, as his name suggests, the romantic of the pack. The reflection of how many real 'Kings of Hearts' I have known who appeared quite literally to *have* four hands helped me to remember his significance very easily. (I'm willing to bet that you won't now forget it in a hurry either!)

The Joker seems to make some people a trifle uneasy, although I have never been able to understand why. Most packs contain two Jokers, so you will need to take one out and throw it away. Take a good look at him too. He is in disguise, masked, pretending to be something he isn't. Now if you look at the meanings page for him (page 115) you will see that he means 'hidden things', in other words, disguises.

Little things like this act as very good memory aids. All the picture cards have little individual differences which you can find for yourself and so supply the necessary prod to your memory.

Before you put your cards away, I suggest that you practise shuffling them. It's very important that they feel comfortable in your hands, and the shuffling practice will ensure that they get thoroughly jumbled up.

3

Basic Preparations

There are 53 cards in your playing card pack — four suits of 13 cards each, and your one Joker.

Each suit — Diamonds, Clubs, Hearts and Spades — covers a different area of life, represents a different season of the year, and is associated with a different set of astrological signs. At this point I would like you to look at the following small chart and to fix firmly in your mind the symbol which represents each suit and the general area of life which that suit covers. You may already be familiar with the symbols, but a surprising number of people are not, and quite a few confuse Clubs and Spades. If you remember that Spades are shaped like old fashioned shovels, that might help.

Diamonds	♦	Practical things
Clubs	♣	Financial matters
Hearts	♥	The emotions
Spades	♠	Obstacles and problems

Once you have these basics fixed firmly in your mind you will find that the cards immediately have some order and clarity for you and this gives you a basis on which to build the next stage.

If you flip to the appendices at the end of this book you will find four sections indexed with these symbols. Each section deals with the indications and generalities of the appropriate suit on its first page, and the detailed meanings of each individual card on the pages following. Each card has been allocated a page to itself, has memory aid drawings, and a Notes section at the bottom. The line drawings are intended to help you to remember the meanings more easily, while the Notes section cuts out the need for you to prepare a separate notebook of your own. You may feel that a card reminds you of something other than my drawings, and this personal

3

reminder can be jotted down in the Notes section.

As you will see, each card has several different meanings, and at first this can be very confusing. Please don't worry about this at present — you will find that, with a little practice, you will know instinctively which meaning will apply in each instance.

When teaching I have found that the best results are gained from keeping the initial tuition as simple and as interesting as possible. For this reason the meanings have been kept brief and to the point and every effort has been made throughout the book to retain your interest by avoiding long and boring lists and explanations. Learning should be *fun* and this learning should be no exception.

Inevitably you are not, at this stage, going to want to memorize all your meanings, but rather to play with your cards and try out little readings — so that is what we are going to do next.

4

The First Reading

When you are ready to attempt a reading, there are — at this stage of interest — just a few basic preparations to be made.

First of all, who are you going to read for? It may be that you have decided that you are going to practise reading on yourself, and I'm afraid that this is not entirely a good idea, and in most cases is virtually impossible. I know of no professional reader who has ever managed to read for themselves with any degree of success. This is because one of the keys to successful reading is objectivity, and it is very difficult to be objective about oneself, with the result that one sees what one *wants* to, not what is actually there.

It is much better if you can practise on someone else, and if they are interested in learning also, allow them to practise on you. Learning is always more interesting if it is done with company, and you may find that you progress more quickly that way. (Don't forget, if you decide to 'learn with a friend', you will need two packs of cards — one each. *You must not share your cards.*)

Having said all this, I am perfectly well aware that the temptation to read for yourself will be very strong, and it is inevitable that you will make the attempt, but I would suggest that you keep these attempts to a minimum.

Even if you decide to share your learning experience, you are still going to need a supply of 'guinea pigs', and frankly this is only too easy. Just telling people of your new interest will produce dozens of eager friends, but a word of caution — casual acquaintances make by far the best practice material. If you read for your best friend, she will inevitably say that you knew all about it before you started, and let's face it she will be quite right. A casual acquaintance about whom you know very little will test your new abilities in a much more satisfactory way — for both of you.

Having found your first 'victim', all you need is a table and two chairs, your cards, and your book open at this page.

4

The *first* thing you should do at the beginning of *every* reading is shuffle your cards really thoroughly and then hand them to your enquirer (the name given to the person for whom you are reading) so that he or she can shuffle them too, before handing them back to you.

In carrying out a reading, the cards are placed in patterns which are called layouts or spreads. At the back of this book I have given just four of the dozens of different spreads in existence, three of which are ideal for beginners and one which is more suitable for those of you who may wish to take this interest further.

I suggest that you start with a One Year Spread, in which one card represents one month of the year to come, with a thirteenth card showing the overall situation.

Detailed instructions for this, your first attempt, are as follows:

1. Shuffle your cards thoroughly.

2. Hand them to your enquirer, who should shuffle them and return them to you.

3. Fan the cards out on the table face downwards. (This takes practice but persevere.)

4. Ask the enquirer to take 13 at random *without turning them over or looking at them*.

5. Remove the remaining 40 cards to one side; you will be reading only from the 13 chosen ones.

6. Take the little pile of 13 cards and, *keeping them in the order in which they were chosen*, lay them out on the table face upward as in the diagram opposite. The first card chosen goes in position 1 and so on.

7. Turn in the appendix to the meaning of card number 13. This contains the overall aspect of the next 12 months, and the area of life in which the most prominent changes will take place, e.g. if this card is a Heart, then the year has a high emotional aspect.

8. Now turn to the meaning of card number 1 which contains the indications for the month in which you are doing the reading — even if that month has only a few days or hours remaining. Go on to card number 2 which is the following month, and so on through the year.

9. You can try joining the sets of three cards in each line together to give you a quarterly (3-monthly) forecast which will help to broaden out the reading quite considerably.

This is a very good practice spread because in the main you are reading the cards individually and need to think only about one at a time. Don't worry if you feel that it is a bit muddled at first. Rome wasn't built in a day, and this is an interest which needs persistence before it pays dividends.

4

4

	13	
10	11	12
7	8	9
4	5	6
1	2	3

4

4

5

Spreads with a Significator

For most types of spreads you will require a card which will, within the reading, represent the enquirer. This card is called the significator and is very useful in showing the attitude of the enquirer to their life in general, and gives a very good focal point to the reading. In spreads which contain a significator the cards falling around it are of prime importance and should always be read first. When you need a significator this should be taken out of the pack before handing the cards to the enquirer for shuffling.

There are two ways of choosing a significator, one by the colouring of the enquirer, the other by his or her birthsign, both of which are outlined by the tables on pages 49 and 50, and you may use whichever method you prefer.

The colouring — hair and skin — of your enquirer, is the traditional method but that can nowadays present problems, particularly if you live in an area of the country which has a high level of ethnic minorities in the community — you could find that using the colouring method means that you will only use one or two of the court cards as the significator, because all the people you see will have the same type of colouring. This is particularly so if you belong to one of the dark-skinned groups of people yourself, when it would be highly likely that all your enquirers would be classed as either Clubs or Spades for the purpose of a reading. Another problem is that the description 'spade' is sometimes applied to black people. I have always hated this, and, having done a great deal of work in the Birmingham area, which has a very high West Indian population, I have never felt able to use a Spade significator for a black client, even when it might have been the most applicable, because it seems vaguely insulting.

According, therefore, to the area in which you live, you may find it more prudent to use the astrology method to find the appropriate card to signify your enquirer. Please bear in mind, though, that whichever method you choose, it is important that you keep to it. Swapping and changing from one to another will only prove confusing and your reading will not be accurate.

5

A good example of a spread containing a significator is the Gypsy Spread, which covers the past, the present, and the future. To help you to get used to the idea of the significator, and to show you its use within a reading, the following are the detailed instructions for the Gypsy Spread:

1. Shuffle your cards.

2. Decide on a significator, either by the colouring of your enquirer, or ask for his or her birthsign. Check the appropriate table on pages 49–50.

3. Take the chosen significator out of the pack and place it face downwards on the table.

4. Hand the remainder of the pack to the enquirer for shuffling and return to you in the usual way.

5. Fan the cards out on the table face down and ask the enquirer to choose 20, again without looking at them, and place them in order in a pile on the table — still face down.

6. Move the remaining cards to one side.

7. Hand the significator card to the enquirer and ask them to place it into the pile of 20 chosen cards *without shuffling them*.

8. Take the 21 cards from the enquirer and lay the cards out face upwards in the order they were chosen, as in the chart below:

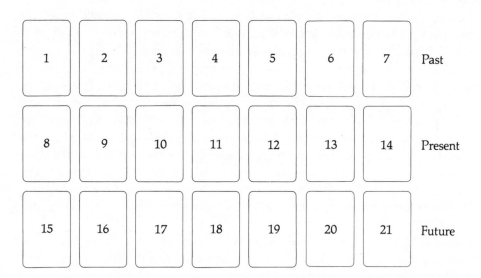

1	2	3	4	5	6	7	Past
8	9	10	11	12	13	14	Present
15	16	17	18	19	20	21	Future

You will see from the chart that the top line covers the indications from the past, the second line deals with the present, and the bottom line shows the trends for the future.

9. Check in which line the significator appears. When the enquirer places the significator in the cards, he or she shows you their attitude to life. If the significator appears in the line indicating the past, your enquirer has a tendency to live in the past, is reluctant to move forward. If it is in the centre line, it can show a tendency to 'live for today', an enjoyment of the present, or it could mean that, again, there is a wariness or fear of what the future may hold. A significator firmly in the line for the future can indicate an eternal optimist, or that the past has been so bad that the enquirer is anxious to move forward. The cards around the significator as well as its actual position in the spread will help you to decide which of these options is the correct one and can give you an insight into how your enquirer is feeling at present.

10. Read the cards around the significator first, then read the meanings for the past, present, and future in that order. Try to tie the cards together in this type of reading, rather than reading each one individually.

This spread will show you clearly how useful a significator can be by giving a definite focal point to the reading, and a useful starting point for you. It is probably the most popular spread used with playing cards because it can give a very full reflection of the enquirer's life up to the present, the future prospects, and how the enquirer is likely to respond to those prospects by his or her attitude.

The third spread suitable for beginners is the Mini Spread, which differs from the other two in that it is not a general spread but is used to focus separately on each individual area in the enquirer's life.

For this spread you should split your pack into the component suits, take out the appropriate significator, and place each suit one at a time face downwards on the table. Ask your enquirer to take four cards from each suit, and to place the significator with one of these sets of four cards.

Remove the remaining cards to one side, and place the chosen cards, still in separate suits, in four squares as below:

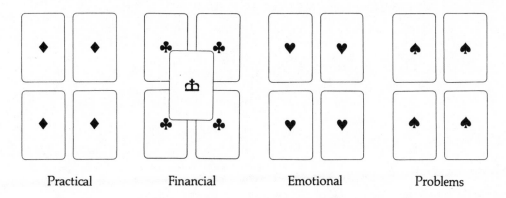

| Practical | Financial | Emotional | Problems |

5

The significator will be with the suit which indicates the area of life which is causing most concern, or is of the most immediate importance to the enquirer. In this example, the significator appears with Clubs, so the main worry is money. In this spread each suit is read individually.

So that you won't have to keep searching around in the book for these three spreads, you will find the basic diagrams and instructions for them, with a fourth spread, at the back of this book.

If you now practise these three spreads on as many different enquirers as you can, you will find that the laying out becomes much easier, and you will get accustomed to handling your cards with confidence. Below are the three general rules which should always be followed when carrying out a reading:

1. Always shuffle your cards yourself at the beginning and end of each reading.

2. Never allow your enquirer to choose from cards which are face upwards. If the faces of the cards are visible, 90% of people will choose those they think are 'good' (some will even choose only red cards) making the reading off-balance and inaccurate.

3. Replace your cards in their box immediately your reading session is over. They should not be left around for others to pick up.

6

Combinations

As you become more used to the cards and have more practice in reading, you will find it useful to broaden the content of the readings by pairing the cards together to create a sequence. In most readings (other than the One Year Spread) you should make the attempt to read the spread cards as a set rather than individually. For instance, you may see a change of job in the cards, but it will be much more satisfactory both to you and to your enquirer if you can see if the job is going to be a success or not. It should then be possible for you to advise how the enquirer can make the most of that success and build on the opportunities provided. On the other hand if the opportunity is not the right one, the cards should show you why, and what else is available. All of this can be achieved — with practice — by looking for a 'theme', e.g. the change of job, and then reading the other cards to enlarge on that theme.

In the Appendix on pages 117–119 you will find a list of the most common pairings. As you gain more experience you will be able to add ones of your own and space has been allocated for you to note these down.

Pairs need not appear right next to each other, but can be anywhere in the spread. Sometimes two or more pairs can be joined together to build a 'story'. For example, you will see from the list that the Ace and the Five of Diamonds appearing together will indicate the purchase of a home. Quite frequently you will also find in the same spread the Ten and Six of Clubs, which together indicate a loan, and would in that instance be the mortgage needed for the house purchase.

One of the commonest pairings is two Aces of any suit, which indicates a mended quarrel. You will quite often find the Two of Spades — a parting — in the same spread as two Aces, showing that that particular parting is only a temporary one.

The more readings you do, the more you will see the possibilities of using these combinations. The ability to link the cards together will show that you are making progress and may be ready to take your interest and your new abilities even further.

Get as much practice as you can, joining in combinations wherever possible.

Memorizing

I'm afraid we have now reached the point where you should make your first attempt to memorize your card meanings; indeed how far you take this interest will depend on how much memorizing you are prepared to do, because this will make your readings much more effective and they will flow much more easily. To achieve this flow you need to be able to look at a card and *know* what it means without referring to the book, or even consciously thinking about it.

You will find that as you use the cards some of the meanings are going to stick in your mind without much effort, but there is no doubt that the feat of memorizing all of them can be very daunting, and this is the time when some students drop by the wayside.

Whether you undertake the memorization or not is up to you. If you want to use this study as just a vague interest you can still carry out fairly effective readings by continuing to refer constantly to your book, and you will get quite a lot of mild pleasure from just 'dabbling'.

However, if you aim to continue with the study and to really improve your readings, then it is essential for the meanings to be firmly fixed in your mind. It is for this reason that the meanings have been kept brief and to the point, and why the memory aid drawings have been put on each page.

Before making any attempt to memorize anything, I would suggest that you put your book firmly on one side, take up your pack, and turn the cards over one at a time. As each one appears try to recite to yourself the various things it can mean. I think you will be quite surprised how much you have taken in just by your initial practising, and your confidence will increase immediately. Put on one side those which you can't remember, check your book, and go through the process again. Keep repeating this until you can go straight through the pack and get them all right. (You are now entitled to treat yourself to a little drink!)

By the way, don't worry if, even after you feel that you know all your meanings,

7

you look at a card and your mind goes blank. It happens to us all, and it soon wears off.

When you have your meanings firmly fixed you can try the fourth spread (page 125). Follow the instructions carefully and take your time with this — it uses your intuitive abilities (which will improve the more readings you do) much more than the other three spreads.

Before I leave the subject of meanings, a word of warning: stick to one set of interpretations — in other words one book. In the past I have had quite a few students come to me for tuition who had previously tried to learn at home. Misguidedly they had bought several books and had taken bits from each one. This made the learning process much longer and much more difficult than it need have been. I am well aware of the motivation behind the 'multi-book' habit — if a reading based on one set of meanings doesn't look too good, it is very tempting to try another set of meanings to see if it comes out any better. From there it is just a short step to adopting all the 'good' bits from each book, so cutting out all potential problems.

In every book on divination the meanings supplied are very carefully balanced to cover every eventuality. Taking meanings from several different sources thus destroys this delicate balance and makes correct learning very difficult indeed.

You must remember that life is comprised of both good and bad, happiness and sadness, success and failure. Frankly, if you can't accept this, you shouldn't be attempting to read cards at all.

8

The Next Steps Forward

(Dos and Don'ts)

There will come a time when you will either decide that you have gone as far as you care to do with this study, or you will begin to find it extremely absorbing. Either way you will not have wasted your time, but, should you at this point decide that this is an interest you want to pursue, then it is also time that you look at the wider implications of what you have started. This inevitably demands that you look very carefully at the responsibilities of becoming involved with the sorting out of other people's problems.

When you first start to read the cards, you will, in all probability, do it for fun, to amuse yourself and your friends. 90 per cent of students start in just that fashion, with a friend and a cup of coffee, with the book to hand for reference. The turning point will come when you produce a reading which hits on a very real and deep-rooted problem within the life of an enquirer, bringing you to an abrupt realization that readings do not deal only with tall dark handsome strangers. Readings can be genuinely accurate, and therefore potentially helpful in the resolution of problems and in giving support and direction. It is at the point of this realization that you will either back away or push forward.

Should you decide to back away you will be doing what thousands have done before you, and what still more will do after you. Most of those who back away do so because they feel a little scared and uncertain about this (to them) unexpected development. Most of them will resume the interest a little later in life, possibly from a different direction.

For the minority who decide to push forward, the action is a very momentous one. It is this pushing action which moves you into a position where your work — for it now becomes more like work — has to be regularized.

You will find that you will, almost without noticing, give your readings more concentrated effort, and that consequently they will become deeper and more

8

accurate. The following guidelines are offered in an effort to help you to avoid some of the more common mistakes and pitfalls.

Your surroundings

Concentration is very much easier in the right atmosphere and you should now aim to read in as quiet a situation as can be managed. The trick, however, with this work is not to go over the top. For instance, some readers insist on working in a completely dark room, lit only by a candle — copied I think from some of the worst type of TV movies. If you find that this is how you work best, then go right ahead, but remember that all that stuffy darkness can seem very weird and scary to your enquirer, particularly if he or she doesn't know you very well. There is also the purely mundane consideration that, if you can't see where you are putting your feet, one or other of you could trip and hurt yourselves. I personally like to see my enquirer, and, although I'm no oil painting, they prefer to be able to see me too, and to watch what I'm doing.

Some readers like to burn incense while working, but this is very much an acquired taste, not shared by everyone, so, as with everything else, moderation should be your aim.

I would suggest that you try to provide a quiet room which is warm and comfortably lit, with a small table and two comfy chairs. Your table should be covered with a dark cloth, kept especially for this purpose. The cloth serves two aims — the cards stand out really clearly against the dark background, and the material helps to stop them slipping about. Velvet is really good for this, but it can be very expensive, so any non-shiny material with a slight nap will do. (Shiny material reflects light and can cause eye discomfort to both you and your enquirer.)

Clothing

Your clothing is a matter of personal taste; some people find that to dress up in either gypsy-type gear or a kaftan is enjoyable and fits the image they are trying to create. Others — like one of the best readers I know — work in jeans and a sweater. If you feel that you like to look the part, or that putting on special clothes helps to get you into the right frame of mind for reading, then by all means do so, but again please remember that your enquirer can be put off by extremes.

What *is* extremely important is that your clothes are comfortable and warm. You will find it very difficult to concentrate on your reading if your belt is cutting you in two or you are shivering with cold. I have some very nice velvety kaftans which I use for exhibition work, partly because they look good, but mainly because they are warm and I can tuck my toes up into the long skirt. Exhibition halls can be very draughty places!

Cleanliness

It does seem rather impertinent to stress cleanliness, but it is important that your

8

enquirer should feel comfortable in the surroundings you create for him or her, and this means that your room should be as clean and tidy as is possible. Remember too that while you are working the enquirer is going to watch you all the time, and they *do* notice things about you. Your hands partiuclarly are on show. A friend of mine going home one evening overheard a fellow traveller give her companion (and the rest of the bus passengers) full details of a visit she had paid to me during her lunch hour, up to and including a description of my clothes *and* the colour of my nail varnish!

Your manner

Please, in your own interests, don't adopt one of those 'out of this world' expressions and the pseudo trance voices. Quite a few readers have found to their chagrin that, far from inspiring respect from enquirers, these affectations are more likely to bring on a fit of the giggles!

From all of these points you will see that I want to dispel from your mind some of the mystique which has surrounded this type of work for far too long. There really is nothing terribly mysterious about reading from cards — those of us who do it every day find it as natural as breathing.

Readings are intended to help people, and you will find that your enquirers will accept the guidance offered by your readings far more readily if they can relate to you as a normal human being, in normal clothes and in pleasant and relaxed surroundings. If you genuinely wish to be of help to people, you must show that you understand their problems, that you are part of *this* world, and that you have both feet very firmly planted on the ground.

Ethics

'My readings lay my life out for me to look at.'

This remark, made to me by a client some years ago, is one of the most apt descriptions I have ever heard. Although some people will have a reading from sheer curiosity, most will look for this method of guidance when they have a decision to make, have reached a crisis point or are just plain depressed.

Objectivity

Because readings are intended to help in a sorting out process they must be totally objective and as clear and compassionate as possible. It is an absolute necessity that you should be able to put yourself into the position of the enquirer, not by becoming involved in their problems, but rather in the way you handle the possible resolution of the problems. In this way you will not tell them anything which you feel would be damaging to them, or to their well-being — in other words you should treat them as you would wish to be treated yourself.

Responsibilities

Any form of psychic development automatically brings additional responsibilities towards the people around you.

It is a great temptation, when just starting this work, to carry out readings as an act of self-glorification — 'look at me aren't I clever?' — rather than as an offer of help to a perplexed fellow human being. You must always remember that — at present — *you are* a human being. Start thinking of yourself as the Second Coming and you really are heading for trouble. This is why you should avoid the temptation to throw out isolated comments in a mysterious way just in order to impress. Rather think of the chain of events you may be starting.

As an example of this type of chain of events, I saw a girl some time ago who

9

came to me because she was very worried about her health. I could see no imminent health problem and told her so. It transpired that, some months previously she had gone to a party and met there — for the first and only time — a woman who was very interested in all aspects of the occult and who claimed to have great 'psychic powers'. The woman told my client: 'You are going to have an illness which will last for several years'. Just that bald statement, given to a complete stranger, issued with an 'I know everything' air, but with no attempt at any form of clarification.

Quite understandably the girl had been extremely worried, and by the time she came to see me was in a state of panic. Thoughts as to how painful this illness would be, would she actually survive it, would she be able to manage financially, would her job be kept open for her, had all been teeming through her mind. The very worst part about this episode was that basically the woman was correct, but she hadn't take her prophecy far enough. There will be an illness for this girl, but not as a *girl*. The illness will be arthritis, will show itself when she is in her late sixties, and will be with her until she dies some years later. This of course placed a different complexion on the whole situation; this girl, like the majority of us, accepts that she will experience bodily wear and tear in later life. What I found totally unacceptable was that she had undergone months of tension and fear simply because one woman wanted to show off.

The lesson behind this is that you should always make your readings as clear and as detailed as possible, and also as kind as is practicable. If you have any doubts at all as to the effects of any part of your reading, then you should keep your mouth very firmly closed.

Behind this obvious lesson, however, lies another and much more subtle one. Why did the woman venture to offer any prophesy when the girl had not asked her to do so? Questioning of the girl revealed that the woman herself had introduced the psychic element into the conversation. In the introduction to this book I refer to looking into the future of those around us 'with their permission and co-operation'. Looking into the life of someone who has not asked us to do so, or even worse, is not aware that we are doing so, *for whatever reason*, is a gross invasion of their privacy, and should not be undertaken under any circumstances.

From this episode, you will see that warnings about illness found in readings need to be treated with great caution, but obviously such warnings, given in time, can be very helpful indeed.

Death

One of the most difficult ethical decisions to make is whether or not you should include death in your readings. Most people fear death, both their own and other people's, so when death is seen in the cards it needs to be dealt with very carefully. I personally tend to gloss over it unless I am asked a direct question about it, primarily because I can see no useful purpose in destroying a person's pleasure in a particular period of their life. Knowing that someone close to you is going to die, particularly if that death is a sudden one, can have exactly that effect.

6

9

All of this may make the undertaking of readings appear to be a veritable minefield, and in a way it is. However I would be failing in my job if I didn't point out to you the possible pitfalls whilst at the same time encouraging you to be as understanding with your enquirers as you can possibly manage to be. Inevitably you will sometimes lose your patience — you wouldn't be human if you didn't. The temptation to shock someone who has openly scoffed at your readings is enormous.

On the reverse side of the coin, people are fascinating creatures, and if you have an interest in them, and adopt a caring and compassionate attitude towards them, you can't go far wrong. Against the self doubts and the sense of responsibility can be weighed the sense of satisfaction. To watch an enquirer go away from you optimistic and relaxed makes all that work and effort well worth while.

6

10

And so to you . . .

But now what of *you*? In the previous chapter I have stressed the fact that your enquirer and his or her well-being is a major factor for consideration, but you too have to get something out of all the hard work which you have put in — and will continue to put in. The sense of achievement which you will get from giving correct and helpful readings will go a long way towards making your work worth while, but the *real* benefits for you will come from your increased development as a person and your increased awareness of the forces around you.

How do readings work?

With that increased awareness and as more of your readings are proved to be accurate, both you and the people around you will begin to question the background to the actual action of reading. In other words, how do the cards work?

I have already described the playing cards as tools. The word tool can have two interpretations in that a tool is an implement with which you work, but it is also an implement which works *for* you — something which implements, or adds to, your own abilities.

The more you use the cards the more they will become an extension of you yourself. You will find that you develop such an affinity with them that the mere act of shuffling them will bring about the increased state of awareness which is necessary if you are to continue with this work in an effective way. This awareness is the opening up of a bridge between your conscious and unconscious mind, making you receptive to the stimulus of the cards. The meanings which you have so painstakingly learned will act as a basis for your thoughts and will in turn trigger other thoughts which will expand as you speak. This is why it is so important for you to memorize your meanings so thoroughly that it is not necessary for you to make the effort of thinking about them. In this way the sight of a card produces an automatic knowledge, leaving the mind free to pursue the thoughts which flood

10

into it. It is this automatic response which shows you which of the meanings you have learned for each card is most applicable.

10

The feat of learning comes into play again when it comes to understanding why the right cards appear. The subconscious mind uses the cards to explain things to you, so the choice of card is dictated by the subconscious in the guise of instinct and in the knowledge of what that card means to you.

For example, using the meanings which you have learned, a move of home would be indicated to you by the presence in the spread of the Five of Diamonds — *because you have learned that that, amongst other things, is what the Five of Diamonds means.* However, if you had fixed it firmly into your conscious mind that a move of house would be indicated by the Two of Spades for instance, then that is the card which would appear in that connection. In other words, it really doesn't matter what meanings you attach to each card as long as the attachment is consistent. As long as your subconscious mind is aware of the meanings you place on each card, it will ensure that the correct ones appear. Now you can see why it is so essential that you should keep to the basics of one set of meanings, rather than confusing your subconscious by working on several sets at once. Look on it if you like as a sort of mental alphabet, with the card meanings building the bridge between the two sections of your mind. The more you use that bridge, the stronger — and therefore the more reliable — it will become.

The list of card interpretations in this book have been carefully balanced to cover every eventuality. However, you will no doubt find that as you use the cards more and more, you will start to adjust and adapt these basic meanings in your own mind, building and expanding on them. This is a normal stage of development, and one you should welcome, because it is a progression, and a sign that your bridge is being strengthened from within, so that the meanings you use will become more and more personal to *you*.

Social Reading

One of the less advantageous aspects of development is that people will try to use you in various ways, and you must guard against this very carefully. I have already said that, once your new interest is known, you will find that you have a steadily enlarging group of friends, all of whom will be only too willing to act as guinea pigs for you. This can develop into a full-time job, and can turn your social life into one long reading. I have lost count of the times I have been invited out to dinner only to find that I am expected to read for all the other guests, so providing free entertainment on behalf of my 'kind' hostess. It is most important that you resist this as much as you can, even to the extent of crossing off one or two of these so-called friends. The difficulty is that, in the first flush of enthusiasm, you may well feel that all this experience is useful to you, and to an extent you will accept any and every opportunity to show off your new skills. Whilst all that practice experience is undoubtedly useful, social reading is a habit which, once formed, is hard to break without causing offence, and I personally feel that it is better not to form the habit in the first place.

10 Absent Readings

You must also resist pressure from your friends to read for someone connected to them who isn't actually there. For instance a female friend may be curious to know what her ex-boyfriend is doing and thinking — particularly if she still fancies him. Absent readings (readings for people who are not present at the time the reading is carried out) are possible and are carried out quite extensively by readers who offer a postal service — as I do myself. However, if an absent reading is to be carried out, it must be at the request of the *person themselves*. It is not ethical for you to carry out a reading simply through curiosity — your own or someone else's — and confronted by this type of request you must weigh up the situation very carefully indeed. In the case of the female and her ex-boyfriend, for instance, you must put yourself into the position of the boyfriend. Would you like someone to probe into your personal life and your feelings without your knowledge? The answer has to be no, and no is therefore the answer which you should give to your friend.

Is the Future Planned Out for Us?

One of the most frequent questions asked by both clients and students is if the future is completely fixed for us. The answer is no, it is not. That can make the action of carrying out readings to be somewhat contradictory, but the explanation is quite simple.

We have choices. Not all the time — but sometimes. This means that on the occasions where there are choices available we can alter our future — and of course the future of those around us — simply by our reaction to change, or by our acceptance or rejection of opportunities in the different areas of our lives.

Readings will show opportunities, and should also show how the enquirer ought to react to these opportunities in order to get the most out of his or her life. The readings will also show straight choices, and in this sphere it is extremely important that the enquirer makes the choices and does not ask you to choose for them. This will happen, and it can create a dilemma for you if you allow it to, so your job is to lay out the options and to make it quite clear that the final choice must rest with the enquirer.

For instance, a reading may show an offer of marriage or it may show an actual wedding. In the case of the wedding *event* showing, your task is easy — you simply read it as a wedding. In the case of an offer of marriage, the situation is much more complex, because the fact that the offer is there does not necessarily indicate that the marriage actually takes place: the enquirer has the option of acceptance or rejection. The task of the reading — and therefore the reader — is to point out the advantages and disadvantages involved, the character of the prospective partner and any opposition that may arise from either family. What is vital is that no opposition or pushing must ever come from *you*. You may feel that you would not touch the prospective partner with the proverbial barge pole, or alternatively that he or she is the best thing since sliced bread, but neither of those feelings, nor indeed any of your personal opinion, must appear in the reading. How the enquirer reacts to the offer is then up to them, and in that way their decision affects the lives of those immediately around them. This dictum of choice on the part of an enquirer and objectivity on the part of the reader must apply to all of the personal opportunities with which the human race is presented.

There are however certain areas of life where there is no choice available — some events *are* planned and are therefore quite unavoidable.

One rather extreme instance of this occurred a few years ago and illustrates the 'planned' situation very clearly — in fact all too clearly. It happened during the first spate of terrorist bombings in the centre of London, when a woman cancelled a restaurant booking at the last minute. When the restaurant was bombed, with a considerable loss of life, she congratulated herself on a lucky escape. Three months later she made an unplanned-spur-of-the-moment visit to another restaurant — and was killed outright when that too was bombed.

One is left with the inescapable conclusion that she was intended to die in that particular way, and that the 'lucky escape' merely put off the inevitable. A reading carried out for her prior to these incidents would have shown both her escape and her ultimate fate. A compassionate reader would have revealed one and not the other — *because she could not avoid it*. This is of course very much an extreme case and the chances of you being confronted with this type of situation within a reading are very slim.

Most of your enquirers will be concerned with much less momentous problems, but they mustn't be treated any more lightly. Remember that what appears to be a small problem to you can appear quite enormous to the person right in the middle of it. Problems tend to grow in the minds of enquirers, too much thinking, too much analysing, causes problems to mushroom out of all proportion and you must be just as interested in the little things as the big ones.

Interest, care, consideration, kindness, objectivity, patience. Such a lot to ask isn't it? Put like that it does seem a lot, but the gains for you are quite frankly enormous. Not financially — even if you eventually decide to offer your abilities for hire, readers very rarely make a fortune. No, the gains are less tangible, and show in the rounding out of your personality, your sense of belonging to the world in a real sense, of knowing who you are and why you are, and most importantly *where* you are in the scheme of things which is loosely referred to as 'life'.

One Final Word of Warning

This type of interest is habit-forming. Once you really get hooked, your involvement will grow very rapidly, and with it your curiosity about life itself.

The interest will become a search for knowledge and truth. It will be enthralling, time-consuming and exasperating, because each new experience, each new solution, will uncover more questions and bring about more probing and more searching by you. It is a search which I, and all those like me, find rewarding and fulfilling.

I hope you will too.

'Wherever I shall walk along the Path of True Knowledge I shall obey my basic instincts in knowing what I must do with the knowledge I have gleaned.

'I shall use nothing to the detriment of my honour or my fellow man. I am not in any way to jeopardize the development of humanity in its set form by what I may know of the future and its outcome.

'This is my honour and my code always.'

From *Ishmael,*
The Keeper of the Seal.

APPENDICES

Choosing a Significator

1. By Colouring of Enquirer

Colouring	Suit
Light blonde, silver hair, pale skin	Diamonds
Warm blonde or light brown hair, warmer skin	Hearts
Dark brown hair, pale or warm skin	Clubs
Black hair, dark skin tones	Spades

Examples

Male enquirer with dark brown hair — King of Clubs

Female enquirer with light brown hair — Queen of Hearts

Notes

2. By Birthsign of Enquirer

Birthdate	Birthsign	Suit
21 March – 20 April	Aries	Clubs
21 April – 21 May	Taurus	Spades
22 May – 21 June	Gemini	Diamonds
22 June – 22 July	Cancer	Hearts
23 July – 23 August	Leo	Clubs
24 August – 22 September	Virgo	Spades
23 September – 23 October	Libra	Diamonds
24 October – 22 November	Scorpio	Hearts
23 November – 21 December	Sagittarius	Clubs
22 December – 20 January	Capricorn	Spades
21 January – 18 February	Aquarius	Diamonds
19 February – 20 March	Pisces	Hearts

Examples

Male Gemini — King of Diamonds
Female Virgo — Queen of Spades

Notes

Diamonds

Season: **Spring**
Astrological attachments: Air signs — **Aquarius, Gemini, Libra**

Diamond cards will cover all the *practical* aspects of life:

Education, intelligence, examinations.
Jobs, careers, business ventures.
Aims and ambitions — both working and personal.
Physical moves of both job and residence.
Travel and hobbies.

Ace of Diamonds

New beginnings

Development of plans and aims.
Large new possession.
New goals and challenges.

Can be used as timing card for **Spring**.

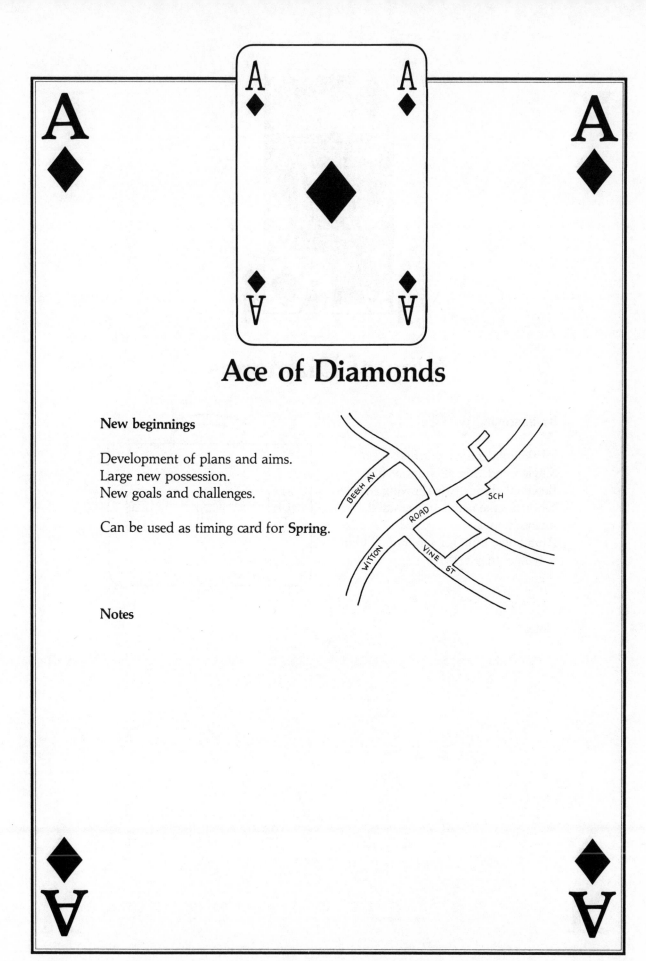

Notes

King of Diamonds

Businessman

Workaholic, puts work first.
Single minded in all areas of life.
Reserved, difficulty in showing emotion.
Tends to take people for granted.
Intensely loyal.
Ambitious, both for self and children
   (where they exist).

Notes

Queen of Diamonds

Organizer

Intelligent, realistic, career-minded.
Organized both at home and work.
Clear sighted — able to give good advice.
Blunt in speech.

Notes

Jack of Diamonds

Boy or immature male
— can sometimes be child of either sex

Quick-witted.
Intelligent.
Bores easily.
Liked by older people.
Very good communicator.

Notes

Ten of Diamonds

Opportunities

Job move to different building.
Change of job due to restlessness.
New working start involving adjustments.
Need for change in all areas of life.

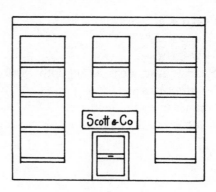

Notes

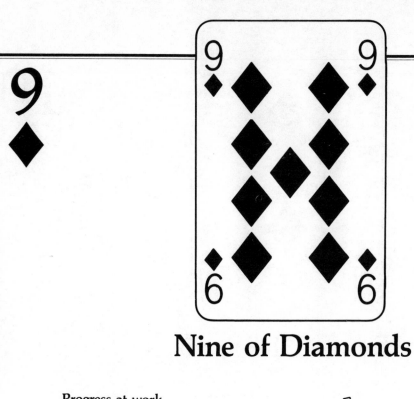

Nine of Diamonds

Progress at work

New interests.
Short journeys connected with work.
New hobbies.
Chance to combine interests with
    increasing income.

Notes

Eight of Diamonds

Indecision

Doubts caused by too much thinking.
Frustrating delays with plans.
Confirmation that delays are
   temporary but necessary.
Holidays.

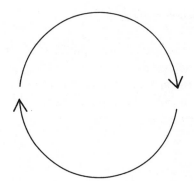

Notes

Seven of Diamonds

Success

Success and achievement based on
    determination.
Sport and hobby satisfaction.
Warning to keep planning simple and
    practical.

Notes

Six of Diamonds

Papers

All papers and letters.
Business work and property documents.
Personal letters and telephone calls.
Examinations and other assessments of ability.
Warning to take care with signing papers.

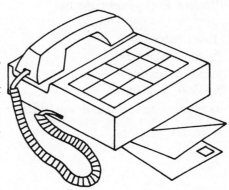

Notes

Five of Diamonds

Practical hopes and potential

House move.
Promotion in work.
Business expansion.
Break from routine.
Increase of knowledge in any form.

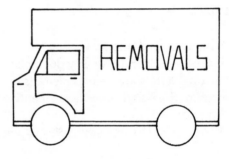

Notes

Four of Diamonds

Doubts

Shelve all decisions at present.
'Wait and see'.
Don't act in anger.

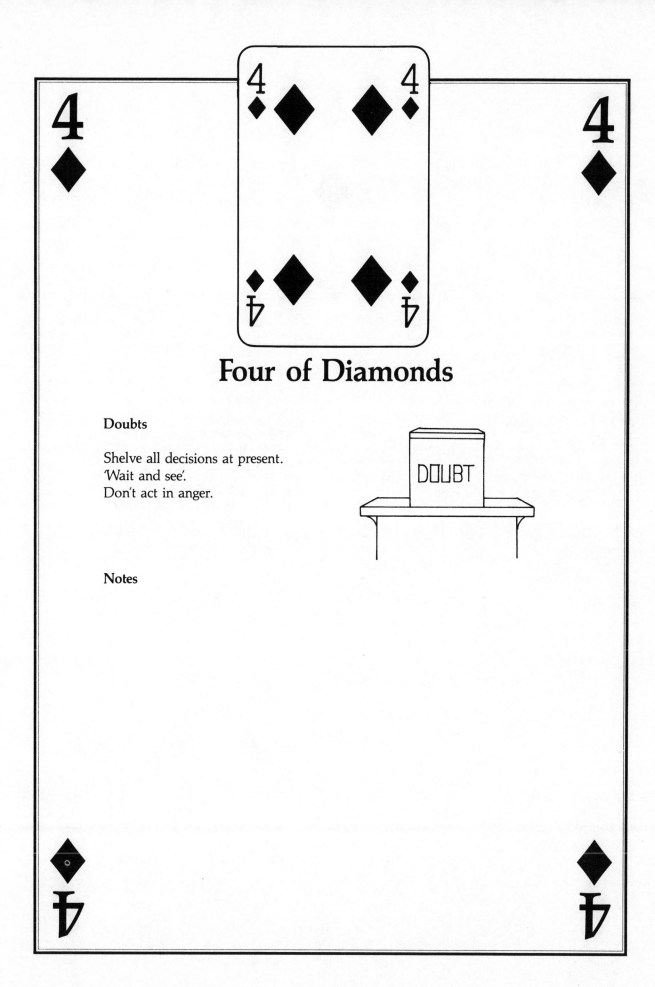

Notes

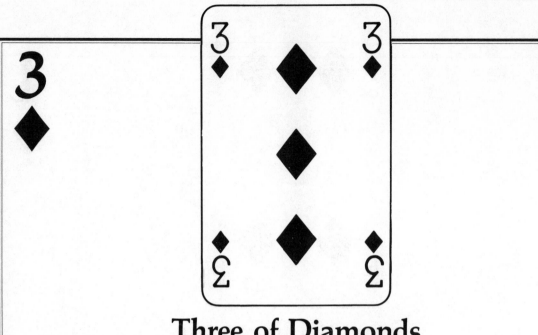

Three of Diamonds

Education

Learning which will increase confidence.
Adjustments to changes of situation.
Adapting to new ideas.

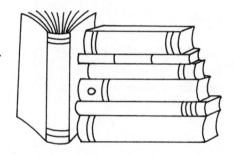

Notes

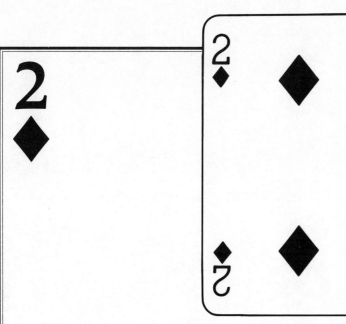

Two of Diamonds

Partnerships

Sharing — responsibilities, home, money
   — with another person.
Working partnerships.

Notes

Clubs

Season: **Summer**
Astrological attachments: Fire signs — **Aries, Leo, Sagittarius**

Club cards will cover all aspects of *finance*, both good and bad:

Increases in income.
Legacies, wins, redundancy settlements, divorce settlements, insurance.
Investments.
Ups and downs of general expenditure.
Personal attitude to the things money can buy.

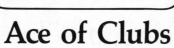

Ace of Clubs

Wage or salary

Increase in income which may not last.
Recognition of a talent which can be used
to make money.

Can be used as a timing card for **Summer**.

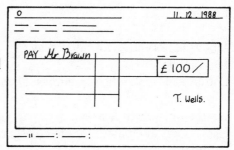

Notes

King of Clubs

Energetic

Enjoys life both at work and play.
Full-blooded.
Enthusiastic male who sometimes shows
    off.
Needs someone to lean on.
Uses money and possessions to create an
    impression.
Can develop a mean streak with age.

Notes

Queen of Clubs

Expensive female

Smart, attractive, well-dressed.
Expects a good standard of living.
Can be snobbish.
Generous when it costs her nothing.
Can be a 'meal ticket' lady — looking for
   a man to keep her.

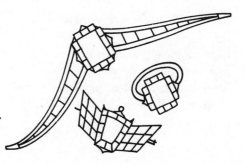

Notes

Jack of Clubs

Boy, youth, or insecure man

Lacking in self-confidence.
Introverted and nervous.
Strong attachment to family or other
   strong influence.

Notes

Ten of Clubs

Lump sum of money

Inheritance.
Settlement.
Redundancy money.
Large win.
(From whatever source should not be
    frittered away but invested.)

Notes

Nine of Clubs

Earned wealth

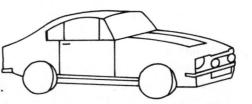

Increase in earning power.
Stability of income offering security.
Settlement money concerned with work.

Notes

Eight of Clubs

Gambling

Small win.
Gambling with both money and
    situations.
Gambling with changes in way of life.

TODAYS RUNNERS	
STAR BOY	3 – 1
ROCKET	6 – 1
JUPITOR	8 – 2

Notes

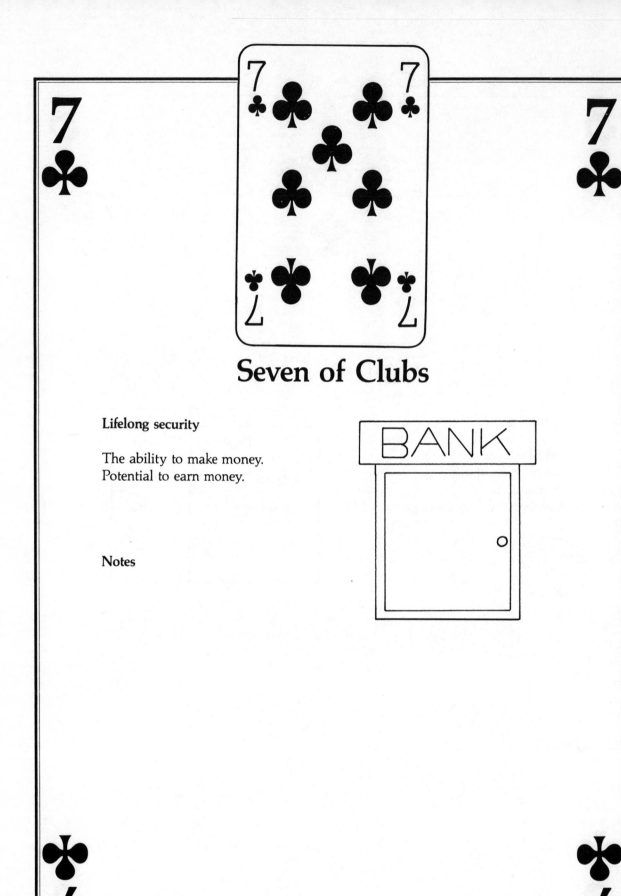

Seven of Clubs

Lifelong security

The ability to make money.
Potential to earn money.

Notes

BANK

Six of Clubs

Money worries

Indicates need for caution.
Warning everything must eventually be
    paid for.
Not to overspend on credit.
Practical help with money, gift, or loan.

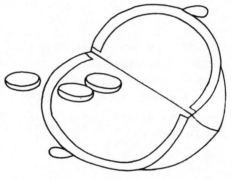

Notes

Five of Clubs

Investments

Investment of time and/or money in
  business or working situation.
Increase of interest on investments.
Increase in work satisfaction with
  increased income.
Shared money.

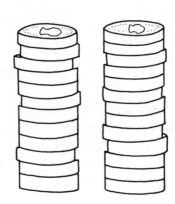

Notes

Four of Clubs

Lack of trust

Warning — take care of personal
    possessions and valuables
Lack of trust from past let down —
    possibly swindled.

Notes

Three of Clubs

Stability

Progress.
Stroke of luck.
Practical help from others.

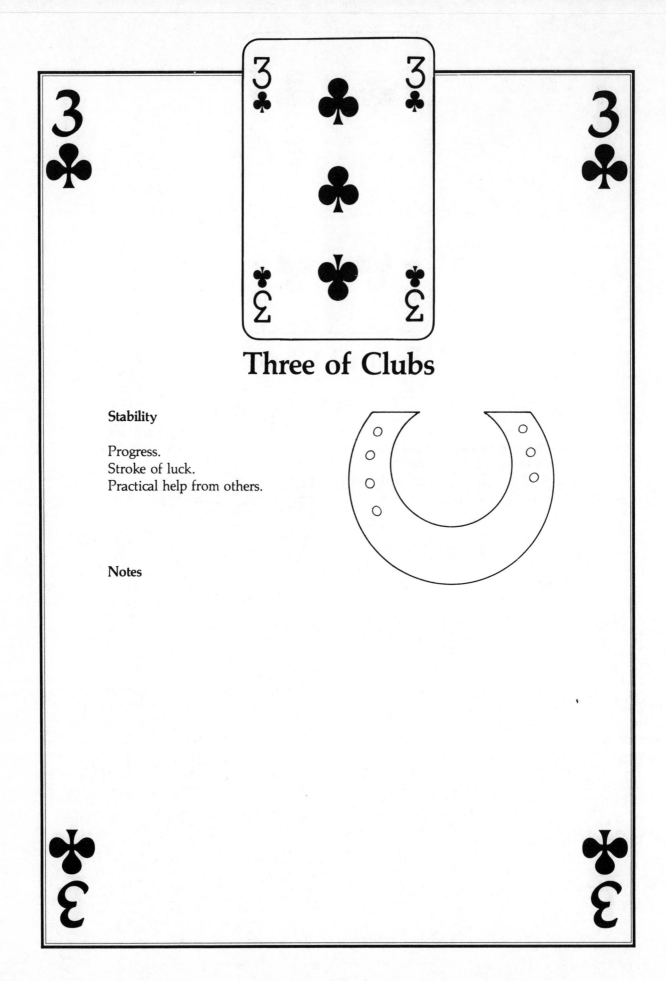

Notes

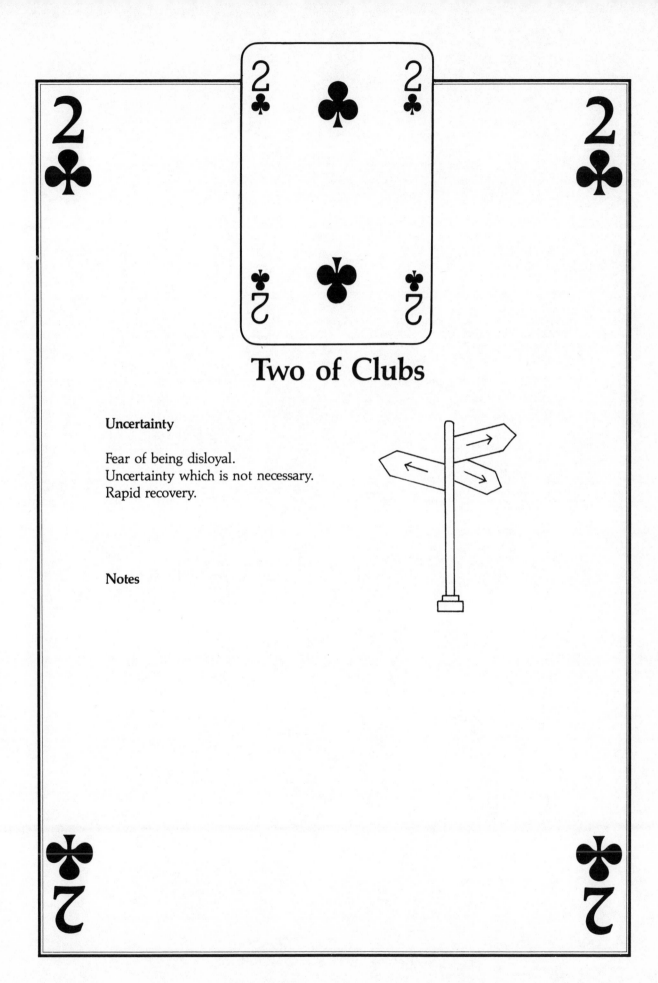

Two of Clubs

Uncertainty

Fear of being disloyal.
Uncertainty which is not necessary.
Rapid recovery.

Notes

Hearts

Season: **Autumn**
Astrological attachments: water signs — **Pisces, Cancer, Scorpio**

Heart cards will apply to all the *emotional* aspects of life:

Family ties and affections
Friends — and enemies.
Lovers, romance, marriage.
All inner feelings, whether expressed or not.
Social events and family occasions.

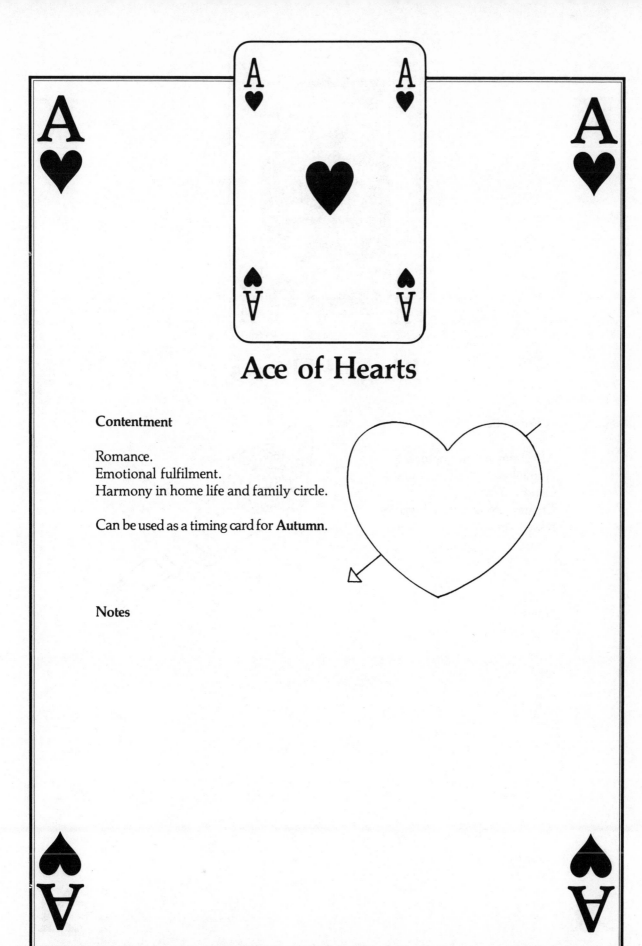

Ace of Hearts

Contentment

Romance.
Emotional fulfilment.
Harmony in home life and family circle.

Can be used as a timing card for **Autumn**.

Notes

King of Hearts

A Romantic

Affectionate and popular.
Home-lover.
Can be artistic.
Creates strong family loyalties.
Likes women.

Notes

Queen of Hearts

Domesticated female

Mother figure.
Affectionate.
Life centres on home and family.
Shy and reserved.
Can be introverted and possessive.

Notes

Jack of Hearts

Immature male — 'Peter Pan'

Reluctant to grow up.
Emotionally insecure.
Mothers boy?
Hurt in past.
Chatter up — safety in numbers.
Unambitious — drifter.

Notes

Ten of Hearts

New emotional beginnings

New relationship.
New phase of existing relationship.
More social contact.
Increased contact with family and old
    friends.
Special family occasion — e.g. wedding.

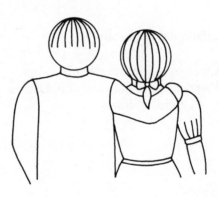

Notes

Nine of Hearts

Emotional opportunity

Offer of stable relationship.
Warning not to play emotional games, or
relationship lost.

Notes

Eight of Hearts

Suspicion

Warning to accept people at face value.
Tendency to look for problems and
   ulterior motives.

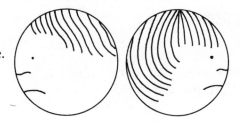

Notes

Seven of Hearts

Fulfilment

Contentment.
Needs still remaining within a
relationship.

Notes

Six of Hearts

Sacrifices

Possible doormat situation —
   domination.
Warning to live life by own needs.
Make own decisions.

Notes

Five of Hearts

Decisions

Choices and decisions about relationships.
Putting down of emotional roots.

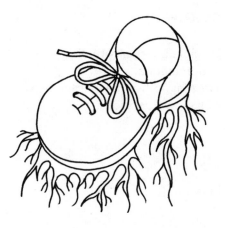

Notes

Four of Hearts

Hurt

Past hurts affecting the present.
Bitterness and resentment.

Notes

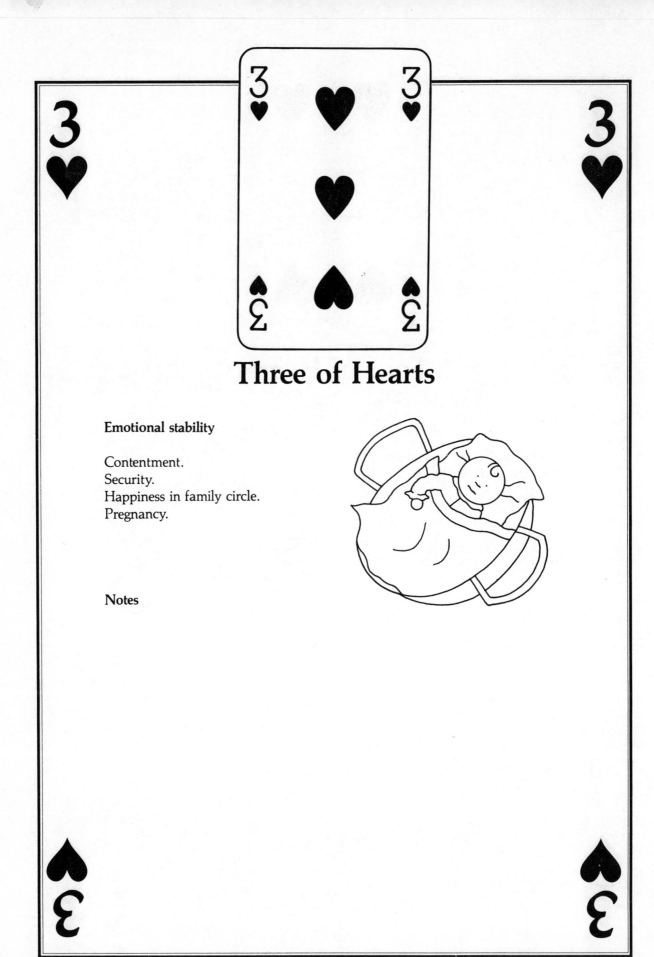

Three of Hearts

Emotional stability

Contentment.
Security.
Happiness in family circle.
Pregnancy.

Notes

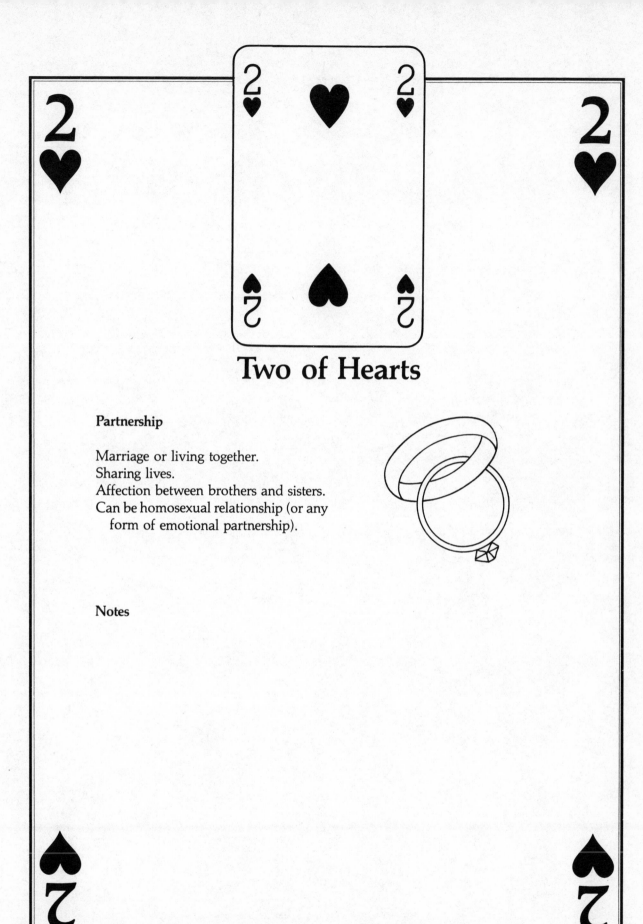

Two of Hearts

Partnership

Marriage or living together.
Sharing lives.
Affection between brothers and sisters.
Can be homosexual relationship (or any
    form of emotional partnership).

Notes

Spades

Season: **Winter**
Astrological attachments: Earth signs — **Taurus, Virgo, Capricorn**

Spade cards will cover *problems and obstacles* in all areas of life:

Depression.
Loss of job.
Broken relationships.
Lawsuits.
Health problems.
Divorce.
Death.

Ace of Spades

Endings

Challenges.
End of chapter of life.
Death.
Legal proceedings.
Can be loss of job/relationship.

Can be used as timing card for **Winter**.

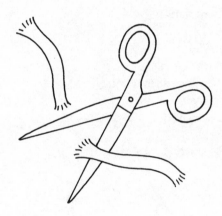

Notes

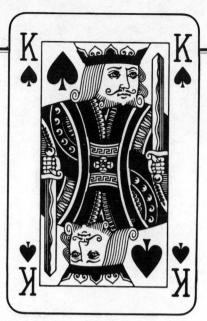

King of Spades

Dominant male

Strict.
Withdrawn.
Afraid of showing feeling.
Bossy.
Defensive.
Jealous.
Possessive.

Notes

Queen of Spades

Two-faced female

Charming but bitchy.
Fond of her own way.
Ambitious.
Not to be trusted.
Possessive.

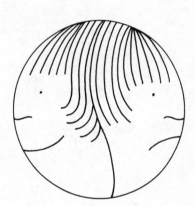

Notes

Jack of Spades

Charmer

False charm.
User.
Deceitful.
Tricky.
Ambitious but lacking ability.

Notes

Ten of Spades

Depressive period

Lack of real movement.
Difficulty in communicating.
Depression.

Notes

Nine of Spades

Worries

General worry.
Warning to curb imagination.
Guard against depression.

Notes

Eight of Spades

Isolation

Loneliness.
Period of isolation — e.g.:
  Hospital stay;
  Prison sentence.

Notes

Seven of Spades

Fear

Groundless fears.
Attempt to understand people better.
Look at both sides of a situation.

Notes

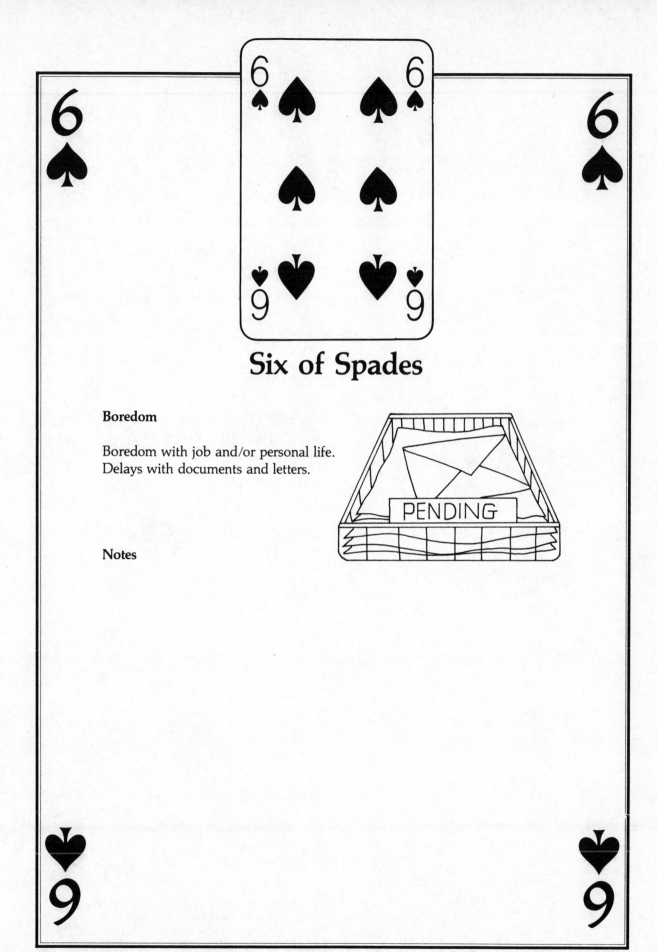

Six of Spades

Boredom

Boredom with job and/or personal life.
Delays with documents and letters.

Notes

Five of Spades

Jealousy

Unpleasant situations.
Friction.
Misunderstandings.

Notes

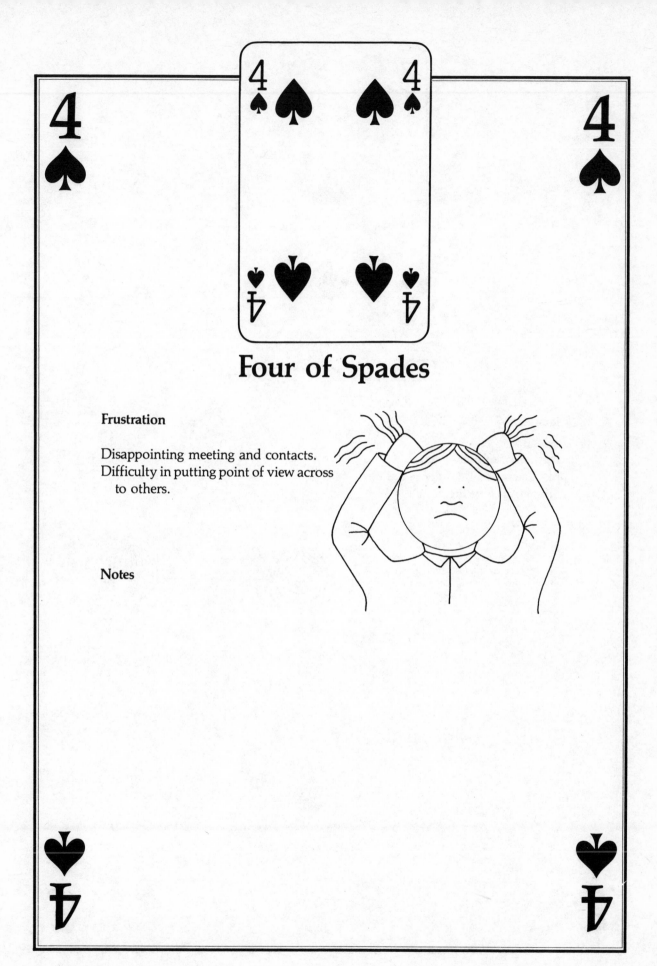

Four of Spades

Frustration

Disappointing meeting and contacts.
Difficulty in putting point of view across
   to others.

Notes

Three of Spades

Interference

Interference in any area of life.
Blocks created by other people.
Triangle in love life.

Notes

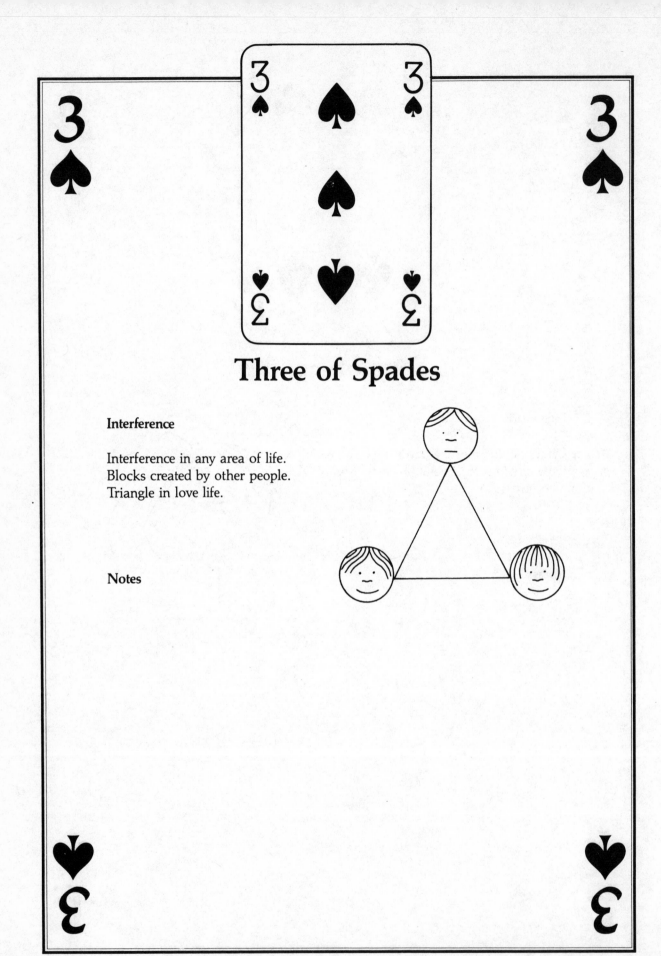

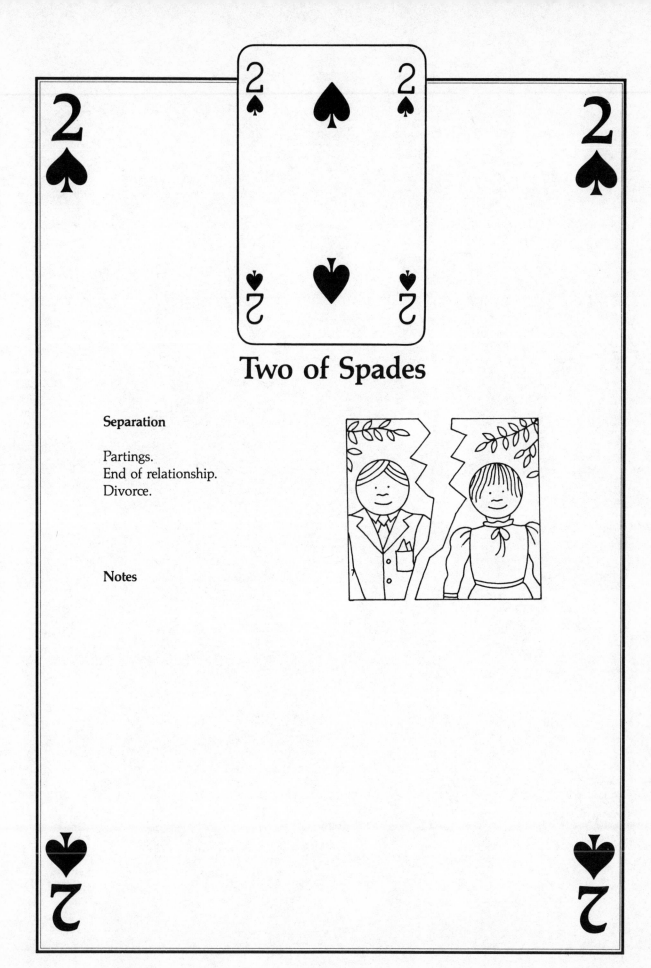

Two of Spades

Separation

Partings.
End of relationship.
Divorce.

Notes

The Joker

Hidden things

Surprising revelations.
Abilities being wasted.
Secrets.

Notes

Card Combinations

Ace of Diamonds with Five of Diamonds
Purchase of new home.

Three of Diamonds with Six of Diamonds
Learning & examinations.

Nine of Diamonds with Ten of Diamonds
Journey over water.

C

Two of Diamonds and Three of Hearts
An offer of marriage.

Two of Diamonds with Five of Clubs
Working partnership.

Ten of Clubs with Nine of Clubs
Lump sum of money as settlement.

Ten of Clubs and Six of Clubs
Taking out a loan.

Eight of Spades and Nine of Spades
Concern about health.

Two Aces of any Suit
Patching up a quarrel.

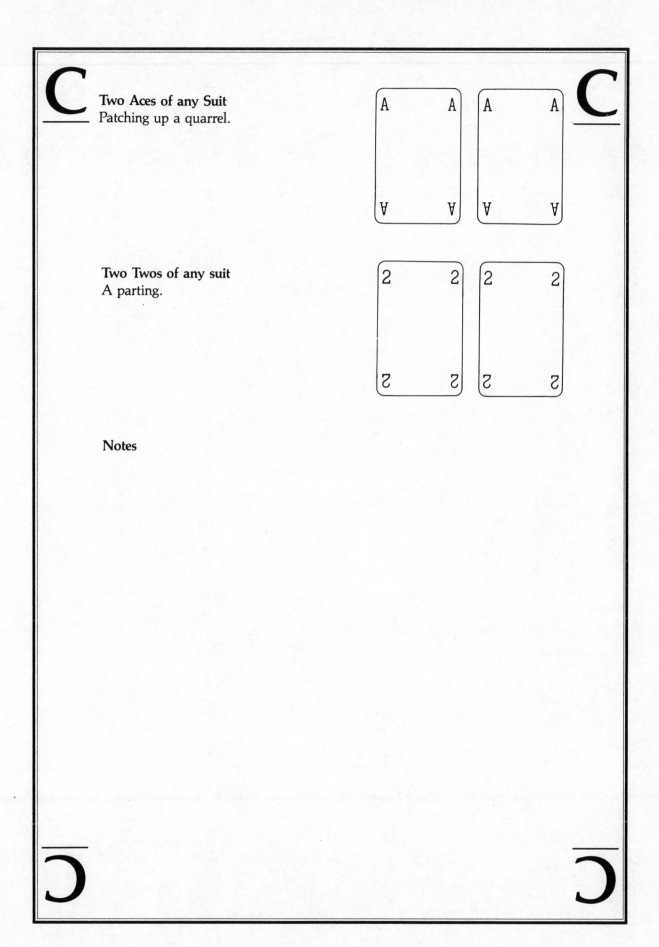

Two Twos of any suit
A parting.

Notes

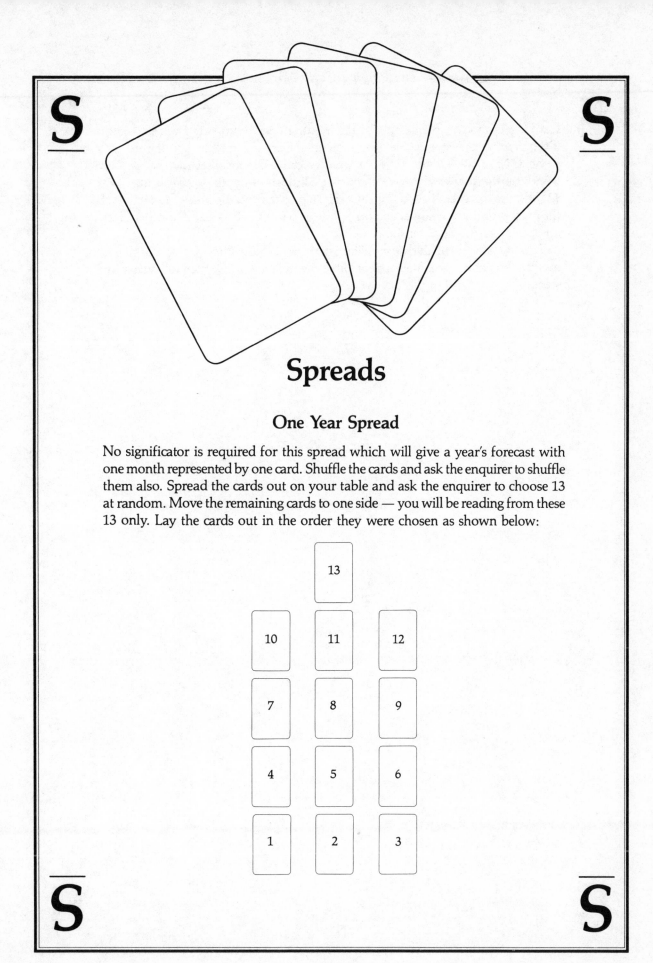

Spreads

One Year Spread

No significator is required for this spread which will give a year's forecast with one month represented by one card. Shuffle the cards and ask the enquirer to shuffle them also. Spread the cards out on your table and ask the enquirer to choose 13 at random. Move the remaining cards to one side — you will be reading from these 13 only. Lay the cards out in the order they were chosen as shown below:

S   **S**

Card 1 contains the indications for the month in which you are reading — even if the month has just a few days remaining — Card 2 is for the next month, and so on to Card 12. As you move through the cards join together each set of three to indicate the quarters of the year and give a little more depth to the reading. Card 13 indicates the overall aspect of the next 12 months and the area of life in which the most prominent changes will take place — e.g. a Club as Card 13 will indicate a lessening of financial tensions.

This spread is particularly useful if carried out in the first few days of the quarter months (January, April, June or September) because it will also then follow nature's seasons.

S   **S**

S S

Gypsy Spread

For Past, Present and Future

Select a significator and then hand the remainder of the pack to the enquirer for shuffling in the usual way. Spread the cards out face down on your table and ask the enquirer to take out 20 at random. Move the remainder of the pack to one side — you will read from these 20 cards plus the significator only. Ask the enquirer to place the significator into the pile of 20 cards, again at random, and then lay out the cards on your table in 3 rows of 7 as shown below:

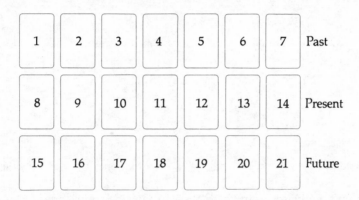

Read the cards in the order of past, present and future, but note particularly the position of the significator. If it appears in the past, the enquirer is reluctant to move forward, is technically living in the past, and the cards in the lines for the present should show you why. If the significator appears in the line indicating the present, the enquirer could be one of those people who 'live for today' and optimistic cards around it will confirm this. However, he or she could be afraid of the future, closing their eyes to inevitable changes. Again check the cards immediately around it. A significator in the line for the future can indicate an eternal optimist, but can also mean that the past and present have not been very kind and the enquirer is anxious to move on to better times. From this you will see that it is always essential to check the cards immediately around the significator as a guide to both character and current state of mind.

S S

S   **S**

Mini Spread

This spread is very useful in giving a mini reading for each individual area of an enquirer's life.

    Remove a chosen significator from the pack. Split your pack into its four suits — place the Joker on one side. In turn, take each suit and spread it out face downward for your enquirer to take four cards from each. Leave the four piles of four chosen cards separate from each other and remove the remaining cards.

    Ask the enquirer to put the significator with one of the four piles. Then turn the cards over as below:

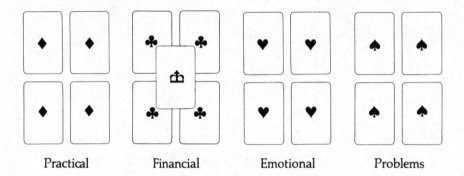

    Practical   Financial   Emotional   Problems

You now have a mini reading which refers to each individual area of the enquirer's life. The significator placement indicates which area of life is of most concern to the enquirer at this particular point in time. Read each small pile separately.

S   **S**

S   S

General Spread

For More Advanced Students

A significator is needed for this spread but is not removed from the pack. Fix the idea of which significator you would choose in your mind, shuffle your pack and ask your enquirer to shuffle also in the usual way. Ask them to place the pack on the table face down and to cut it into two piles and then to cut each pile into two again (four piles should now be on the table). Turn the piles over so that you can see the top card of each one and read these four from left to right.

Pick up each small pile in turn and find the significator you had already decided on. Read only from the pile containing the significator, the remaining three piles can be put on to one side. Place your cards out in rows of six as below (use all the cards in your hand even if you cannot make up complete rows of 6):

Sometimes you will have just a few cards to work with, sometimes there will be a great many depending on the way the enquirer cuts the pack. If the significator is on the end of a row ask your enquirer to take another card at random from the ones you discarded and place it by the significator. The significator card must always be surrounded by other cards, your enquirer should take as many from the discards as is needed to do this. For example:

S   S

*Extra cards taken from discards

Read the cards around the significator first. Then allow your eyes to wander over the other cards and read whichever one takes your eye. This takes practice, but you can achieve a nice smooth reading in this way and it is surprising how quickly you learn to relax and follow your instinctive judgement as to which card should come next.

Because this spread deals almost exclusively with the future it is a very good spread to use to show general indications and trends and should cover approximately the next six to nine months.

Suggested Further Reading

Bernard, Graham,   *Why You Are Who You Are* (Destiny Books, 1985)

Butler, W.E.,   *How to Develop Clairvoyance*, (The Aquarian Press, 1968)

Cooke, Grace,   *The New Mediumship* (The White Eagle Publishing Trust)

Peach, Emily,   *The Tarot Workbook* (The Aquarian Press, 1984)